NIGEL
SLATER

30-MINUTE SUPPERS

PENGUIN BOOKS

PENGUIN BOOKS

Published by the Penguin Group. Penguin Books Ltd, 27 Wrights Lane, London w8 5TZ, England. Penguin Books USA Inc., 375 Hudson Street, New York, New York 10014, USA. Penguin Books Australia Ltd, Ringwood, Victoria, Australia. Penguin Books Canada Ltd, 10 Alcorn Avenue, Toronto, Ontario, Canada M4V 3B2. Penguin Books (NZ) Ltd, 182–190 Wairau Road, Auckland 10, New Zealand · Penguin Books Ltd, Registered Offices: Harmondsworth, Middlesex, England · The recipes in this edition have been selected from *Real Fast Food*, *Real Fast Puddings*, and *The 30-Minute Cook*, first published in hardback by Michael Joseph in 1992, 1993 and 1994 respectively. This edition copyright © Nigel Slater 1996. All rights reserved · The moral right of the author has been asserted · Typeset by Rowland Phototypesetting Ltd, Bury St Edmunds, Suffolk. Printed in England by Clays Ltd, St Ives plc · Except in the United States of America, this book is sold subject to the condition that it shall not, by way of trade or otherwise, be lent, re-sold, hired out, or otherwise circulated without the publisher's prior consent in any form of binding or cover other than that in which it is published and without a similar condition including this condition being imposed on the subsequent purchaser
10 9 8 7 6 5 4 3 2 1

CONTENTS

For A B
My best friend for almost twenty years

Introduction

This is a collection of recipes for everyday eating: simple food that is easy to prepare and quick to cook. It is written for anyone who enjoys good food eaten informally, and should particularly appeal to those who lack the time to cook it. Most of the recipes are based on fresh food with as little as possible done to it. There are no complicated procedures, no dithering around with affected arrangements on over-sized plates, and no effete garnishes. It is a set of straightforward recipes for fast food with bold flavours, cooked in minutes and served without pretension.

The recipes are easy and within the grasp of all but the most ham-fisted of cooks. While most of the recipes included here are fast, I make no claims for five-minute feasts or ten-minute dinner parties. I think that good food can be measured only by its flavour and freshness, not by a stop-watch. That said, most of the recipes in this book can be completed in under 30 minutes, which is, after all, the time it takes a supermarket cook-chill supper to heat through. Many of them take just half that time. The ingredient lists are short and most of the recipes require only one or two fresh ingredients that can be bought on the way home. I like the idea of buying one ingredient that looks particularly good, then mixing it with some storecupboard staples and seeing what happens.

Fast food is not just about pizzas, hamburgers and noodles, good though they can be; fast food can also mean a slice of truly ripe Charentais melon eaten with a hunk of salty Feta cheese and a few black olives, or perhaps a juicy white peach sliced and dropped into a glass of chilled deep yellow wine.

Think of a piece of chicken brushed with aromatic herbs and lemon, then char-grilled and stuffed into a crisp roll slathered with garlic mayonnnaise, or a comforting bowl of porridge with blackberries and heather honey. Imagine shredded peppery basil leaves stirred into buttery mashed potato, a slice of pork pan-fried with fennel or a plate of purple-yellow muscat grapes and ripe figs. All this is fast food.

Whether it is Mrs David's immortal omelette and a glass of wine, a hot bacon sandwich when you return from the pub on a cold night, or a plate of pasta with slices of soft white goat's cheese and leaves of pungent fresh thyme, there is nothing like real, fast, food.

TROUT IN A FRESH HERB AND LIME CRUST

The fresh herbs and citrus juice here work together to lift the slightly dull flavour of farmed trout. Use lemons if you don't have limes, and any suitably delicate herbs.

FOR 2, AS A MAIN COURSE

4 large trout fillets, skin removed
3 limes
60 ml/4 tablespoons mixed, chopped herbs: parsley,
*   tarragon, dill*
30 ml/2 tablespoons fresh breadcrumbs
salt
25 g/1 oz butter

Check that all the bones have been removed from the fish by running your fingers over the flesh and remove any stubborn ones. Finely grate two of the limes and add their zest to the herbs and breadcrumbs. Add a little salt.

Melt the butter in a small pan and add the juice from the two grated limes. Put the herb mixture on a flat plate and press the fillets down firmly on one side. The herbs will stick to the fish. Place the fillets on a baking sheet and spoon over the lime butter.

Bake in a preheated oven at 200°C/400°F (gas mark 6) for 6 minutes. Serve with crisp green beans and the remaining lime cut in half.

TROUT SALTIMBOCCA

Trout needs a bit of help nowadays. It has lost much of its joy now that it is so intensively farmed, yet it still jumps into people's shopping baskets at an alarming rate. Here is a way to lift it from its doldrums, based on the traditional Italian way with veal, though inspired by the brilliant Alastair Little, who uses red mullet.

FOR 2, WITH NEW POTATOES AND SALAD

85 g/3 oz cold butter
4 large slices of Parma ham
2 large trout, weighing about 450 g/1 lb each, filleted
4 large sage leaves
a little plain flour
groundnut oil for frying
juice of 1 lemon

Cut the butter in two and cut one half into 4 thin slices. Lay a slice of Parma ham flat on the table, place a slice of butter in the middle, then put one of the trout fillets on top. Roll up the fish in the ham, place a sage leaf over the loose end and secure with a cocktail stick.

Season the flour with salt and pepper. Heat a thin layer of oil in a frying-pan. Dust each parcel thoroughly with flour. Place, butter side down, in the pan and cook for about 3 minutes, till the ham is crisp. Turn over with the help of a fish slice, and cook for a further 2 minutes.

Remove to a hot plate. Tip the juices from the pan. Melt the remaining butter over a high heat and, as soon as it starts to froth, add the lemon juice and a little salt and pepper. Pour the hot, frothing seasoned butter over the fish and serve immediately.

RED MULLET WITH FENNEL AND PERNOD

A wonderfully light dish for a summer evening, where the fish is perfumed with fennel bulb and a glug of Pernod. A chilled rosé, perhaps one from Provence, and some olive bread would complete the picture.

Red mullet has a high ratio of bone to flesh, so if you hate struggling with fish bones, ask your fishmonger to fillet the fish and reduce the cooking time by half.

FOR 2, AS A MAIN DISH

2 red mullet, cleaned, livers intact
salt
freshly ground black pepper
2 heads of fennel, about 125 g/4 oz each, trimmed
1 small onion, sliced
15 ml/1 tablespoon olive oil
Pernod

Season the mullet inside and out with salt and pepper. Shred the fennel finely, and sweat it with the onion in the oil in a shallow pan until it starts to soften, about 5–7 minutes. Try not to let it colour, which will coarsen the flavour of the dish. Put the sweated mixture in a gratin dish to form a bed for the fish. Lay the fishes on the fennel, add a good glug from the Pernod bottle, or use Ricard if that is what you have. Bake in a preheated oven at 180°C/ 350°F (gas mark 4) for 20 minutes, until the fish is firm and tender. 5

Salmon is a fish rich in oil. When cooked, it needs something piquant to offset this, particularly if grilled, but less so if poached. Lively partners include salty olives, sharp sorrel, tiny green-tinged tomatoes and peppery basil.

Your salmon steaks for grilling should be no more than 2.5 cm/ 1 inch thick. They need little lubrication, having enough of their own oil. Brush each steak with a small amount of oil, olive for preference, just enough to glisten but hardly enough to be seen. Set them under a very hot, and I mean very hot, grill. Set the grill pan about 10 cm (4 inches) away from the heat.

Cook the steaks until the flesh is firm but springy. At 2.5 cm/ 1 inch thick this will take barely 4 minutes a side, but test them after 3. Transfer them to a warm plate. Don't forget to scoop up the pan juices.

Good things to serve with Grilled Salmon

Basil Butter

Cream 125 g/4 oz butter in a bowl. This is easier if the butter is at room temperature first. Chop up a little shallot and stir it into the butter. The shallot is not essential, so no matter if you haven't one. Shred a small handful of basil leaves. Stir them into the butter with a pinch of salt and a good squeeze of lemon. Chill in the fridge until you need it. Drop a spoonful on to the hot salmon as you serve it.

Black Olive Butter

There are two ways to make a good olive butter. Either whizz a handful of stoned black olives, an anchovy fillet or two and a clove of garlic in the blender till smooth, then mix in about 50 g or a couple of ounces of softened butter. Alternatively, if time or temper forbid even that, stir a spoonful of black olive paste from a jar into an equal amount of softened butter. Either way, serve a dollop of it, as chilled as you can get it, on the hot salmon as you serve.

Quick Cherry Tomato Sauce

Cut 200 g/7 oz cherry tomatoes in half. Scoop out the seeds and discard them, or add to a vegetable stock later. This won't take as long as you think it will. Chop the tomato flesh and scoop it into a small bowl. Add 30 ml/2 tablespoons fruity extra virgin olive oil and a splash of white wine vinegar. If you have any fresh herbs – tarragon, basil or coriander – now is the time to throw a tablespoon of the chopped leaves in too. Taste the purée, add salt and white pepper if you wish, then spoon over the salmon.

Sorrel Sauce

Sorrel, thanks to the marketing men, now comes in Cellophane packs in the supermarkets. Its sharp lemon notes are just what is needed with the salmon. Melt some butter in a small frying-pan and drop in a handful of washed sorrel leaves. Stew them in the butter for 4 or 5 minutes. Stir. They will have melted into the butter. You have a sauce.

GRILLED PRAWNS IN YOGHURT AND LIME

Goa, or at least parts of it, is pretty much my idea of paradise. Especially out of season. Anywhere that has tall palms, long beaches with only me on them and straw huts to sleep in is my kind of place. They can still be found if you know when and where to go. But I am not going to tell you. I can stand any number of lazy days in the sand and sea and long, stoned evenings interrupted only by supper. The seafood is good too. I probably ate more prawns in a few weeks than I usually eat in years. The price has a lot to do with it. A few rupees buys what would cost a few quid back home. My fishmonger has cooked (pink) and uncooked (grey) prawns, though he is one of the few, so I usually have to make do with cooked. A not-too-expensive treat if you munch a filling naan, warmed under the grill, at the same time.

FOR 2

450 g/1 lb large (but not huge) prawns in their shells
2.5 cm/1 inch knob of fresh root ginger, grated on the coarse side of the grater
2 cloves of garlic, crushed to a paste
5 ml/1 teaspoon garam masala
2.5 ml/½ teaspoon chilli powder
15 ml/1 tablespoon ground coriander
grated zest of a lime (use the fine side of the grater)
15 ml/1 tablespoon lime juice
125 ml/4 fl oz thick yoghurt

Thread the prawns on to long stainless steel or wooden skewers.
8   It won't take long and will save time later, when you come to turn

them. Mix together all the other ingredients with a teaspoon or so of salt and lay the skewered prawns in it. Leave them there for 15 minutes, or longer if you have time.

Get the grill hot – use either one of those grill pans that sit on top of the gas or an overhead grill. Remove the prawns from the marinade (some of the gunge will come with them) and cook them on each side for 4 minutes. It is worth remembering that they are already cooked (if they were pink), so the cooking time is very short. The prawns are ready when they have caught a little on the grill and are juicy inside their shells.

Remove the prawns from their spears as you eat, sucking the shells clean before peeling them back to get at the juicy meat within.

THAI GREEN FISH CURRY

A green curry from Thailand, rich with coconut and fragrant with basil and coriander. Keep the heat low, though it may still curdle a little. That is its nature. You can use a ready-made curry paste but your own will be fresher tasting and can be made in a couple of minutes. You can use a few slices of lime instead of the lime leaves at a push but they aren't really the same and leaves are not so difficult to find. Two out of three of my local supermarkets have them.

FOR 2, WITH RICE

450 g/1 lb fish steaks or thick fillets
1 × 200 g/7 oz block of creamed coconut
45 ml/3 tablespoons Thai Green Curry Paste
(page 18)
6 kaffir lime leaves

> *5 ml/1 teaspoon fish sauce* (nam pla)
> *15 ml/1 tablespoon chopped coriander leaves*
> *30 ml/2 tablespoons chopped basil leaves*

Cut the fish into large bite-sized pieces. Don't cut it too small, no matter how small you may think your mouth is. Cut the creamed coconut into chunks and dissolve it in 300 ml/½ pt hot water. Bring the coconut milk gently to the boil, in a heavy-based saucepan, stirring almost constantly. Stir in the curry paste and turn down to a gentle simmer.

Add the pieces of fish, the lime leaves, a good pinch of salt and the fish sauce. Simmer gently for 12 minutes, until the fish is cooked. Taste for seasoning – you may like to add more salt. Scatter over the chopped coriander and basil leaves and serve, with rice if you wish.

POACHED SKATE WITH THAI FLAVOURS AND ITS BROTH

A soothing way to eat a meaty wing of skate, served with a gently aromatic broth made interesting by some of the signature notes of Thai cooking: coriander, ginger, lemon grass and chilli. It does not have to be skate, I am sure a hunk of hake would be fine too, but the gelatinous texture of the skate seems to make the broth even more comforting. Serve with bread.

FOR 2

> *2 skate wings*
> *a lime, sliced thinly*
> *2 kaffir lime leaves*

2 cloves of garlic, squashed flat
2 hot red chilli peppers
2.5 cm/1 inch knob of fresh root ginger, peeled
2 spring onions, chopped
1 stalk of lemon grass, bruised
8 black peppercorns
chopped coriander leaves
dark soy sauce

Place the skate wings in a large shallow pan such as a straight-sided frying-pan. Pour over enough cold water just to cover and add the lime slices and leaves, squashed garlic cloves, chilli peppers, the ginger cut into coins, the spring onions (both green and white bits) and the lemon grass. Season with peppercorns and a little salt.

Bring slowly to the boil over a medium heat, turn the heat down and leave to simmer – shudder is probably a better word – for 10–15 minutes, or until the fish has firmed up. Don't overcook it – the fish is ready when opaque, wobbly and easy to break into strands with a fork.

Sprinkle with fresh coriander leaves and shake in a little soy sauce to taste. Serve in an old-fashioned soup plate or similar deep-rimmed plate with some of its poaching liquor. Drink the sustaining, aromatic broth first and then attack the fish.

CRUMBED AND PAN-FRIED SCALLOPS WITH
PARSLEY AND LEMON

The rich person's answer to fish fingers. A lemon and garlic butter, flecked with parsley, is as near as we get to tomato ketchup. But a tomato salad, scattered with olive oil and black pepper, would make a quick accompaniment.

FOR 2, AS A MAIN DISH WITH A SALAD OR VEGETABLES

1 clove of garlic, crushed
finely grated zest of ½ lemon
45 ml/3 tablespoons chopped flat-leaf parsley
85 g/3 oz butter, at room temperature
freshly ground black pepper
8 large juicy scallops, cleaned
1 egg, beaten
fresh breadcrumbs
butter and groundnut oil, for frying
2 handfuls of mixed salad leaves

Mix the garlic, lemon zest and parsley into the butter. Season with the black pepper. Dip the scallops in the beaten egg, then roll them in the breadcrumbs.

Heat enough oil and butter to measure one finger's depth in a shallow pan. When hot, slide in the scallops and fry till the crumbs are golden and crisp, about 3 minutes on each side. Place the salad leaves on 2 plates and put the hot scallops on top. Throw the oil and butter out of the pan, add the lemon and parsley butter and warm for 30 seconds. Spoon over the scallops and serve.

CHICKEN WITH LEMON AND OLIVES

Chicken simmered slowly with spices, onions, lemons and olives is an ancient Moroccan dish. I first came across it in a restaurant in Marrakesh, hidden down an alleyway. A rather dubious alleyway, now I come to think of it. This is my version, bastardized for the sake of speed. Mine lacks the intensity of flavour you can only achieve by marinating the chicken overnight (in a slightly lighter mixture), from simmering slowly for a couple of hours, and using preserved lemons. But I think my version wins on texture (in traditional versions the chicken falls apart) and perhaps tastes somewhat more lively. A sprinkling of parsley wouldn't go amiss.

FOR 2

2 plump cloves of garlic, peeled
10 ml/2 teaspoons paprika
10 ml/2 teaspoons ground cumin
2.5 ml/½ teaspoon ground black pepper
60 ml/4 tablespoons olive oil
4 butcher's chicken thighs, or 6 supermarket ones, on the bone
1 medium onion, finely chopped
5 ml/1 teaspoon saffron threads
10 ml/2 teaspoons ground turmeric
125 g/4 oz green olives, stoned
2 large lemons

Crush the garlic cloves to a paste with a little salt. Mix with the paprika, cumin, black pepper and half the olive oil. Toss with the chicken and leave as long as you can.

Heat the remaining olive oil in a shallow casserole. Add the chicken pieces and cook on all sides till golden. Lift the chicken out with a draining spoon and add the onion, with a little more oil if it is getting low. Cook, stirring from time to time, till golden, and then add the saffron, the turmeric and the olives. Cook over a medium heat for 2 minutes and then return the chicken to the pan. Pour over the juice of a lemon and 225 ml/8 fl oz cold water. Slice the second lemon and add to the pan. Bring to the boil, cover with a lid and then simmer till the chicken is cooked, about 15 minutes, basting regularly.

You need about 75 ml/5 tablespoons of spicy sludge per person; if too much liquid remains, boil hard to reduce it slightly. (You may well find you do not need to.) Check the seasoning, adding salt if necessary, depending on how salty the olives are. Serve the chicken with the sauce spooned over. And with rice pilaf if you wish.

GRILLED CHICKEN WITH MUSCAT WINE AND THYME

These chicken pieces will be especially delicious if you let the sweet wine caramelize slightly on the skin as they grill. Use an orange muscat wine, such as Essensia or Brown Brothers for a change, drinking the rest of the bottle with nuts and fruit afterwards. I serve this dish with sautéed potatoes and a blood orange and watercress salad.

FOR 2

1 small carrot
1 small onion

> *a stick of celery*
> *4 cloves of garlic, lightly crushed*
> *the leaves from a few fresh sprigs of thyme*
> *2 wineglasses of muscat wine*
> *4 chicken pieces, breasts or thighs*

Dice the carrot, onion and celery. The pieces should be about the size of dolly mixtures. Toss them together in a bowl with the garlic cloves, thyme leaves and muscat wine. Put in the chicken pieces and turn them over in the wine. Set them aside whilst you prepare the rest of the meal.

Heat the grill, place the chicken pieces on the grill pan and set them about 10 or 12 cm/4 or 5 inches from the heat, a little further if they have a bone in them. Spoon over plenty of the herb and wine juices and grill for about 12 or 15 minutes, turning once and basting with the wine. They are ready when the juices from the chicken run clear and the skin is golden and crisp. Spoon the wine and herb juices over the chicken as you serve it.

PLAIN GRILLED CHICKEN

I find it difficult to think of anything I would rather eat than a piece of chicken that has been grilled over an open fire. I wouldn't choose a breast, much more likely a boned and flattened leg. It will have been brushed with a little olive oil, seasoned with coarsely ground black pepper and grilled over embers, its flesh juicy and its skin slightly charred. The only addition would be half a lemon on the side of my plate.

In the summer, when I can cook and eat my food out of doors, something as simple as grilled chicken is a popular supper. In the winter I have to resort to cooking on my grill indoors. Like most domestic grills, I guess, this is one where the heat comes from above. It does not give quite the same effect as this most ancient of cooking methods; the food lacks the smoky tones from the aromatic embers, and great care has to be taken to stop the food drying out. I find that continually basting with an aromatic oil or butter keeps the food juicy and fragrant.

I am convinced chicken tastes better, and is somehow juicier, when cooked on the bone. Of course it takes longer to cook through. A little care is needed to avoid the skin being reduced to cinders in order to cook chicken right through to the bone. Set the meat a good 10 cm/4 inches from the heat source and almost double up on the cooking time; expect a leg or breast to take about 20–30 minutes to grill, turning once. To check whether it is cooked don't spear the flesh with a skewer as that method loses all the precious juices. You must pinch it, between thumb and forefinger. Firm and springy – it is probably ready; soft and squashy – almost certainly not.

Four ways with Grilled Chicken

Grilled Chicken with Herb and Shallot Butter

Mix together, in a food processor if you like, 85 g/3 oz butter, a small handful of fresh breadcrumbs, 2 finely chopped shallots, 1 clove of garlic and 30 ml/2 tablespoons parsley. Spread the paste over the chicken 5 minutes before it is due to finish cooking. Baste regularly.

Grilled Mustard Chicken

When you brush the chicken with oil, brush it also with a couple of heaped tablespoons mustard, the crunchy Dijon variety for preference. Grill as usual.

Teriyaki Chicken

Before you grill the chicken pieces, leave them in the following mixture for as long as you have time for, then keep brushing them with it throughout their spell under the grill: 50 ml/ 2 fl oz groundnut oil, 50 ml/2 fl oz shoyu soy sauce, 1 finely chopped garlic clove, 30 ml/2 tablespoons *mirin* (sweet rice wine) and the grated zest from a small orange.

Honey and Soy Grilled Chicken

Mix together 30 ml/2 tablespoons runny honey with 15 ml/ 1 tablespoon each light soy sauce and lemon juice. Sprinkle in a few drops of Tabasco sauce, and 1 crushed clove of garlic. Brush the chicken pieces with the honey and soy mixture and grill as before, brushing regularly.

QUICK GREEN CHICKEN CURRY

The lime leaves are available in cute little packets from good supermarkets and in bunches from oriental grocers. They are essential here. I have found nothing else that will give the unique tart freshness they contribute. A beautiful, highly fragrant supper.

350 g/12 oz boned chicken breast
350 ml/12 fl oz coconut milk
15 ml/1 tablespoon groundnut oil
30 ml/2 tablespoons Thai Green Curry Paste (see below)
8 kaffir lime leaves
45 ml/3 tablespoons basil leaves, shredded

Cut the chicken into large bite-sized pieces. Gently bring the coconut milk to near boiling, but do not let it do so. In a shallow-sided pan, fry the chicken pieces in the oil till golden, about 2 minutes over a high heat. Stir the curry paste into the coconut milk, add salt and the lime leaves. Pour the warm, spiced coconut milk over the chicken and simmer, very gently, for 12 minutes. Scatter over the shredded basil leaves. Their peppery scent will rise immediately.

THAI GREEN CURRY PASTE

I love green curries, especially the ones scented with basil or coriander, but have always avoided making them as I thought the green curry paste would be time consuming and the ingredients impossible to find. Wrong. It actually takes all of 10 minutes (and 9 of those are peeling the lime, and chopping the garlic, ginger and shallot) to make this lively, hot, versatile paste.

There is one, and only one, ingredient in this hot, fresh-tasting mix that you will not find in a decent supermarket: galangal. This knobbly, pinkish tuber looks like a cross between a ginger root and the flag irises in my garden. Its gingery, peppery, lemon flavour is hard to simulate, but Thai friends assure me it is not the end of the world if you miss it out. Their trick in desperate moments is to add ginger and a little lime juice instead. If you are passing, it is available in (or usually outside) oriental greengrocers, where it can also be bought dried. Occasionally I have seen it at branches of one of the major supermarkets.

> 6 medium-hot green chilli peppers, about 5 cm / 2 inches
>   long, seeded and chopped
> 2 stalks of lemon grass, chopped
> 30 ml / 2 tablespoons chopped coriander leaves (and its
>   root if possible)
> 5 ml / 1 teaspoon ground cumin
> 2.5 cm / 1 inch knob of fresh root ginger, peeled and
>   chopped (if you can get galangal, use it)
> 2 shallots, finely chopped
> 5 ml / 1 teaspoon coriander seeds
> 3 cloves of garlic, finely chopped
> 5 ml / 1 teaspoon black peppercorns
> 5 ml / 1 teaspoon chopped lime zest
> 15 ml / 1 tablespoon lime juice

Whizz to a paste in a blender, adding a little more lime juice if it sticks.

• *Now that you have made the paste you can use a little for either of the following recipes; store the remainder for up to a week in a screw-top jar in the fridge.*

MOZZARELLA CHICKEN WITH PESTO GRAVY

I have given two methods for the same dish. The first gives a neater result, while the second, which I think the more interesting, is not for the faint-hearted. It includes turning the chicken over in the pan so that the cheese topping melts into the pan juices, resulting in a deeply savoury finish.

FOR 2, AS A MAIN DISH WITH A SALAD

2 large boneless chicken breasts
50 g/2 oz butter
30 ml/2 tablespoons groundnut or vegetable oil
45 ml/3 tablespoons pesto from the jar
1 ball/125 g/4 oz of Mozzarella cheese, cut into 5mm/
¼ inch slices
freshly ground black pepper

Cut each breast in half lengthways and flatten with a rolling pin between two sheets of clingfilm, until they are 5 mm/¼ inch thick. Be gentle, you don't want a purée. Cook the chicken in the melted butter and oil in a shallow pan for 1–2 minutes on each side.

Without removing the chicken from the pan, spread each piece with a tablespoon of the pesto sauce, place a slice of Mozzarella on top of the pesto and sprinkle with pepper. Now, EITHER:

pick up the chicken with a fish slice and place it in a grill pan. Flash under a preheated grill till the Mozzarella melts. Add the remaining pesto to the pan with 50 ml/2 tablespoons water and stir. Remove the chicken from the grill and pour over the pan juices, OR:

20   turn the chicken over with a palette knife so that the cheese is

on the bottom. As soon as it starts to melt and sizzle, scoop each piece up with a fish slice, making sure that the melted cheese is not left behind. Turn the chicken over, the cheese and pesto now tantalizingly melted, and place in a warm serving dish, easing the cheese from the slice with a palette knife. Add the remaining pesto and 30 ml/2 tablespoons water to the pan, in which some of the pesto and cheese will be left behind, and stir, scraping up all the crusty bits in the pan. Pour the pesto pan juices over the chicken and eat immediately.

LAMB CHOPS WITH ONIONS, MUSTARD AND CHICK-PEA PURÉE

A robust way to eat grilled lamb with red wine, caramelized onions and mustard, with a chick-pea mash to drizzle the mustardy gravy over.

FOR 2

1 large or 2 medium onions, peeled
15 ml/1 tablespoon olive oil
1 × 400 g/14 oz tin chick-peas, drained and rinsed
a sprig of thyme
2 cloves of garlic, peeled and left whole
4 small or 2 large lamb chump chops
50 g/2 oz butter
45 ml/3 tablespoons Greek-style yoghurt
90 ml/6 tablespoons red wine
30 ml/2 tablespoons grainy Dijon mustard
30 ml/2 tablespoons chopped parsley

Cut the onions into segments from stalk to root, to give 8–10 wedges of onion. Separate the layers and cook with the oil over a medium heat in a shallow pan. Empty the chick-peas into a pan and cover them with water. Throw in the thyme and garlic. Salt, and simmer for 15 minutes.

When the onions are soft, translucent and starting to brown at the edges push them to one side of the pan and turn up the heat. Place the chops in the pan and cook on both sides till the fat is golden and crisp, the meat browned and the insides pink and juicy. Probably about 4 minutes on each side. Meanwhile, drain the chick-peas, remove the thyme, and mash with a potato masher. Stir in the butter and yoghurt. Season with pepper. Lift the onions, which should be soft with slightly crisp edges by now, and the lamb on to warm plates.

If there is more than a film of fat in the pan, pour it away. Pour in the red wine, scrape any crusty bits from the pan with a wooden spatula, and set over a high heat till half of the wine has evaporated, a matter of a minute or two. Stir in the mustard and most of the parsley. Season with salt and pepper, and simmer for a minute or so till thoroughly hot. Spoon the sauce over the chops and onions. Scatter over the remaining parsley.

PORK CHOPS WITH TARRAGON AND WHITE WINE

Aniseed notes are rather good with pork. This classic French way with pork is very much the sort of thing I hope to be offered on a plain white plate on a plain white paper cloth in a roadside café. But rarely am.

FOR 2

a large knob of butter
15 ml/1 tablespoon groundnut oil
2 large or 4 small pork chops
30 ml/2 tablespoons tarragon leaves
125 ml/4 fl oz white wine – not too dry
another large knob of butter

Put the butter, a lump about the size of a whole walnut in its shell, into a frying-pan with the oil. You can use olive oil if that is what you have. As soon as it is hot but before it starts to smoke, add the chops. Cook them over a moderate heat until both the meat and the edges of the fat have browned on each side, which should take about 5 minutes on the first side and 3–4 on the other. I don't know why it takes less time to cook the second side, I only know that it does.

Pour out any excess fat from the pan, season the chops with salt and ground black pepper, and scatter over the tarragon leaves. You can chop them if you like but there is little point. Pour in the wine and simmer, covered with a lid, for a couple of minutes more, turning once. Remove the chops to a warm place, turn up the heat under the pan and boil until the liquid has reduced to a little more than a couple of tablespoonfuls; then add the second knob of butter, a little smaller than the first. Swish round the pan till it sizzles, and pour over the chops.

• *A plate of green veggies, dark green ruffle-leaved Savoy cabbage or green beans cooked till slightly floppy, would be my choice of accompaniment here.*

LAMB'S LIVER WITH MUSTARD AND MADEIRA GRAVY

Piquant flavours – here capers and mustard – perk up a piece of liver like nothing else. A 10-minute meal this one, except that I really think it is at its best with some buttery mashed potatoes or, even better, a mash of half potatoes and half parsnips, which will, of course, take you well into 30 minutes. Noodles, cooked in 10 minutes and tossed in softened butter and garlic, are a quicker option.

FOR 2

280 g/ 10 oz lamb's liver, thinly sliced
a little plain flour
50 g/ 2 oz butter
125 ml/ 4 fl oz Madeira
1 wineglass of red wine
10 ml/ 2 teaspoons capers, rinsed
15 ml/ 1 tablespoon grainy French mustard

Coat the liver lightly in flour. Melt half the butter in a shallow pan and when it stops foaming add the liver. Cook over a medium heat for about 1 minute per side, a little longer if your liver isn't as thin as it might be. Lift out the liver to a warm plate and then pour in the Madeira and the red wine.

Reduce the liquid over a high heat till half of it has evaporated. Stir in the capers and the mustard, and a little black pepper and salt. Stir and leave to bubble for 2 minutes. Replace the liver, and any juices that may have run out. Cook for a minute longer and then serve.

24

SOUVLAKIA

I virtually lived off these spicy parcels, bought for the equivalent of a few pence, and wrapped in thin, slightly greasy pitta, when I used to spend a month each summer in Greece. They were copiously spiced with onion and hot pepper, with a slick of thin sour yoghurt to drip through the fingers, rendering them deliciously lickable.

FOR 2

350 g/12 oz cubed lamb
1 medium onion, peeled
50 ml/2 fl oz olive oil
4 cloves of garlic, peeled
5 ml/1 teaspoon ground cumin
5 ml/1 teaspoon cayenne pepper
4 pitta breads
60 ml/4 tablespoons yoghurt
a little chopped raw onion and a sprinkling of cayenne
*   pepper, to serve*

Put the lamb into a deep bowl. Whizz the onion to a mush in a food processor or blender with the oil, garlic, cumin, cayenne and a good grinding of black pepper. Scoop the spicy slush over the lamb cubes. Toss them around a bit. Set aside for as much time as you have. An hour is ideal, though 15 minutes is better than nothing.

   Heat the grill. It should be very hot so that the outside of the lamb crisps nicely before the inside is more than pink. Shake any excess marinade from the cubes, then grill till slightly charred but still juicy inside – you will have to test one to see, but it will take 25 about 4–6 minutes on a hot grill tossing them about from time to time to get all sides cooked.

Sprinkle with salt, stuff them into a pitta bread, or not, and drizzle yoghurt over them. Sprinkle the top with chopped raw onion and a dusting of hot cayenne.

SAUSAGE WITH LENTILS

Sausage with lentils is one of the most satisfying dishes imaginable. Tinned lentils are a possibility, though somewhat pointless here as small green or brown lentils do actually cook in less than 30 minutes. Just.

FOR 2

125 g / 4 oz small brown or green lentils, such as those
  from Le Puy
85 g / 3 oz pancetta or smoked bacon
1 small onion, finely chopped
100 g / 4 oz brown mushrooms, chopped
1 large clove of garlic, sliced
30 ml / 2 tablespoons chopped parsley
4 plump pork sausages, spicy Italian ones or best
  butcher's

Rinse the lentils in a sieve in running cold water. Cut the pancetta or bacon into small cubes and fry in a deep pan till the fat runs. If it fails to, in other words if your bacon was too lean, then add a tablespoon of oil. Fry the onion in the fat for 4–5 minutes till it starts to soften and then add the mushrooms and the garlic. Stir, cover with a lid and cook for 5 minutes.

Add the lentils and enough boiling water to cover them by an inch or so (about 600 ml/1 pint). Cook over a moderate heat for 20 minutes, then test for doneness. They will probably need another 5 minutes. Season with salt and black pepper, and stir in the parsley. Meanwhile, fry the sausages till they are done to your liking. I suggest at least 20 minutes over a moderate heat with a bit of fat. When the sausages are brown and tender, turn up the heat under the lentils to evaporate most, but not all, of the liquid, while you slice the sausage. Serve them on hot plates on a bed of the lentil and mushroom mixture.

- *Italian grocers, and some supermarkets, sell spicy Italian sausages. Even the one they call mild is spicier than ours. Don't eschew the type sold in vacuum packs, they are surprisingly good, and usually very juicy. Unopened, they will last for a couple of weeks in the fridge, though check the sell-by date. I find them a little too garlicky as a breakfast sausage.*

PAPPARDELLE WITH MOZZARELLA, GRILLED PEPPERS AND OLIVES

The contrast between the tender noodles and crisp breadcrumbs is what makes this dish for me. The dressing is a piquant mixture of lemon, capers and olives and makes the whole thing sing.

FOR 2

225 g/8 oz dried pappardelle
3 bottled red and yellow peppers (they usually come in halves, in which case you need 6)
90 ml/6 tablespoons extra virgin olive oil

juice of ½ lemon
15 ml/1 tablespoon capers, rinsed
chopped flat-leaf parsley
4 anchovy fillets, rinsed and chopped
90 ml/6 tablespoons fresh breadcrumbs
50 g/2 oz butter
1 ball of Mozzarella cheese, cubed
a handful of stoned black olives

Cook the pappardelle in boiling salted water for about 10 minutes till tender. It should be slightly tacky, not slimy.

Meanwhile, rinse the bottled pepper pieces under a running tap to remove their bottling liquid. Cut them into strips and place in a grill pan. Drizzle them with half of the olive oil and grill till sizzling. Pour the juices from the pan into a bowl. Beat in the remaining olive oil with a fork or small hand whisk and add the lemon juice, capers, parsley and anchovies, and season with black pepper.

Cook the breadcrumbs in the butter in a shallow pan. They should turn golden within 5 minutes or so. Stir them so as not to let them burn. Drain the pasta and return to the pan. Toss with the golden crumbs, grilled peppers, Mozzarella cheese, olives, and dressing. Serve warm, rather than hot.

PASTA WITH GRILLED TOMATOES AND ONIONS

Grilling the tomatoes and onions gives the sauce a wonderful, caramelized flavour. But there is nothing subtle about this dish. It is one I value on cold autumn evenings when I am in search of sweet robust flavours and something that will stand up to a bottle of cheap red wine.

SERVES 2

5 large tomatoes, very ripe
15 ml / 1 tablespoon thyme leaves, chopped
salt
freshly ground black pepper
olive oil
280 g / 10 oz dried pasta
2 medium onions, sliced into rounds, about
    5 mm / ¼ inch thick
2 cloves of garlic, very finely chopped
Parmesan cheese, to serve

Slice the tomatoes in half and scoop out the seeds. Put them, skin side up, in an ovenproof dish in a grill pan and scatter them with half the thyme and a little black pepper and drizzle them with olive oil. Set under a preheated hot grill and cook until the skins blacken and smell sweet – about 4–6 minutes.

Cook the pasta in boiling salted water until it is *al dente*. Remove the tomatoes from the ovenproof dish and place the onion slices, drizzled with olive oil and the rest of the thyme, under the grill. Turn them once as they cook. They should be soft and browned at the edges – about 6–7 minutes. Chop the tomatoes roughly, charred skins and all, and throw them in a pan with the grilled onions, their oil and the garlic. The easiest way to chop the tomatoes is to use a knife and fork or to whizz them briefly in the blender. Add the garlic and simmer for 2 minutes.

Season with salt and some more black pepper. Drain the pasta and stir in the tomato, onion and oil. Be generous with the Parmesan.

PASTA WITH WHOLE GARLIC, GOAT'S CHEESE AND THYME

When garlic is cooked whole, the cloves lightly crushed, at a low temperature for a long time, it takes on a deep, sweet flavour. Its fragrance is warm and soft and makes this a dish truly for all the senses.

You will need fresh thyme too; no, not dried, fresh. A little Cellophane packet from the supermarket will be enough. The garlic takes about 25 minutes to cook, so don't attempt it if you have only 10.

FOR 2, AS A MAIN DISH

a large head of garlic, the cloves plump and pink
50 ml/2 fl oz extra virgin olive oil
about 6 healthy sprigs of thyme
175 g/6 oz dried pasta
175 g/6 oz crumbly white goat's cheese

Separate the garlic cloves. Crush each one lightly by pressing down hard with the flat of a knife blade or the heel of your hand, which will loosen the skins. Pop the cloves out of their papery skins.

Pour the oil into a small pan and add the garlic. Cook over a gentle heat for 20–25 minutes, until the cloves are tender, golden and sweet. They must not burn or they will turn horribly bitter.

Strip the thyme leaves from their branches and add them to the garlic, 15 minutes after it has started cooking. Cook the pasta in boiling salted water until it is *al dente*, drain and toss gently with the olive oil, garlic cloves and thyme. Crumble the goat's cheese and stir in.

PLAIN WHITE RICE

Exactly what it says. Serve as an accompaniment or as a main course if you are feeling decidedly delicate.

FOR 4, AS AN ACCOMPANIMENT

175 g/6 oz long-grain white rice
5 ml/1 teaspoon salt

After weighing the rice, tip it into a measuring jug. Note the quantity, then pour it into a heavy-based saucepan. Add the salt, then add exactly twice the quantity of cold water. This will probably be 400 ml/14 fl oz.

Bring to the boil, turn the heat down to a simmer, then cover with a lid. Cook for 12 minutes, no longer. Lift the lid: there should be no water left and little steam holes should have appeared in the rice. Lift a few grains of rice out with a fork, taste them to see if the rice is tender. It probably is. Replace the lid and remove the pan from the heat. Leave for 2 minutes.

Good things to stir into Rice

My favourite rice is the fragrant basmati, which is pertinent to this book because it cooks quicker than some. I have had little joy from the boil-in-the-bag instant rices that I somehow manage to overcook even when I stick to the instructions like glue. I much prefer to wait slightly longer for basmati. Rice reheats reasonably well, at least better than pasta, and it may be worth cooking a little extra, cooling it quickly and keeping it in the fridge for the next day. I have reheated many a bowl of rice in a colander over boiling water then tipped it into a bowl and stirred in something savoury from the cupboard.

There are times when a bowl of steaming rice, perfumed basmati or pure and comforting white, is simply enough. When this is the case try stirring in one of the following aromatic mixtures.

- Lots of butter and Parmesan cheese
- Sliced mushrooms, sautéed in butter with a teaspoon ground coriander
- A handful of toasted pine nuts
- A tin of lentils, drained, well-rinsed and warmed with a knob of butter
- Hot spinach, shredded and cooked beforehand in butter
- Shavings of Pecorino cheese and shredded raw fennel
- A spoonful of black olive paste and a couple of finely sliced, sun-dried tomatoes
- Tarragon leaves and a spoonful of tarragon vinegar
- Shredded carrot, toasted flaked almonds and raisins
- Thin shreds of ham, Italian Parma or Spanish *serrano*, or cubes of cooked smoked pancetta
- Cubes of smoked bacon, cooked crisp, stirred in with their hot fat
- A tablespoon extra virgin olive oil and a dash of balsamic vinegar
- A lump of commercial garlic and herb soft cheese
- Herb butter and a squeeze of lemon juice
- A handful of chopped mint, and half a cucumber, peeled and diced

- A rich, buttery cheese, such as Brie or Taleggio, cut into cubes
- A spoonful of basil pesto from a jar
- Finely chopped chilli peppers and chopped fresh coriander leaves
- A spoonful of spicy *harissa* sauce

FRESH PLUM TABBOULEH

The sumptuousness of ripe plums, the nutty bulghur grains and the refreshing notes from the mint and lemon produces a salad of myriad flavours and textures.

FOR 4, AS AN ACCOMPANIMENT, OR 2, AS A
  LIGHT LUNCH

85 g/3 oz bulghur wheat
50 g/2 oz (a good handful) flat-leaf parsley
25 g/1 oz mint
juice of 2 lemons
30 ml/2 tablespoons olive oil
salt
freshly ground black pepper
4 small spring onions, trimmed
225 g/8 oz (about 6) perfectly ripe juicy plums

Cover the bulghur wheat with cold water and leave for 15 minutes. Chop the parsley and mint finely. Place in a salad bowl with the lemon juice, olive oil, salt and a few grinds of pepper. Chop or snip the onions into small pieces.

Halve each plum, pull or cut out the stone, and toss them into the herbs and dressing. Squeeze the water from the bulghur wheat with your hands. Drop the grains into the salad bowl and then mix gently with the plums and herbs.

BAKED FETA WITH THYME

Even the most mundane of corner shops seem to stock plastic-wrapped planks of Feta cheese. More sophisticated stores may also sell Halumi, a similarly salty white cheese most often found in Cyprus. Although firmer and saltier than the norm found in Greece, they can be turned into a good supper with a little olive oil, some crusty white bread and a glass or three of red wine, as rough as you like.

FOR 2

200 g/7 oz block of Feta or Halumi cheese
15 ml/1 tablespoon olive oil
2 healthy sprigs of thyme leaves

Cut the cheese into two thick slices using a large knife. Place each slice on a piece of kitchen foil, dribble over the olive oil and scatter over the thyme leaves.

Put the cheese under a preheated hot grill or in a hot oven, 220°C/425°F (gas mark 7), very loosely wrapped round the foil, and cook until the cheese is warm and soft and slightly coloured here and there, 7–10 minutes. Eat with crusty bread and perhaps a tomato and cucumber salad.

Cheese counters, in supermarkets and delicatessens, are often the home of really good cheese. A slice or two cut from a whole cheese and picked up on the way home can make a substantial snack, especially if following a bowl of soup. Well-made farmhouse cheeses, as opposed to shrink-wrapped factory blocks, respond to careful matching of accompaniments and the right glass of wine.

Six ways with Cheese Plates

Taleggio with Grapes and Walnut Oil

Taleggio is a delicate Italian cow's milk cheese, usually found in its red-and-white-paper-covered grey rind. It is slightly firmer than Brie. Choose a little more than you think you will need, as its rind is not good to eat, and anyway the paper sticks to it. Lay a slice, about 1 cm/½ inch thick, on a plate, scatter over a handful of halved and seeded black grapes and then drizzle with a little walnut or gentle olive oil.

Gorgonzola with Warm Potato Salad

Lay a 1-cm/½-inch slice of ripe Gorgonzola on a plate. Accompany it with a potato salad made by slicing warm boiled new potatoes in half, mixing them with a few torn rocket or spinach leaves, then tossing in a little olive oil and lemon.

Feta with Raw Peas

Cut a slab of Feta in half horizontally. Drop a handful of shelled raw peas (available ready shelled from some major supermarkets) over the salty white Greek cheese and drizzle with extra virgin olive oil.

Farmhouse Cheshire with Walnuts and Pears

A good farmhouse Cheshire takes some beating. Put a wedge, large enough for one, on a plate. By its side lay a ripe pear, sliced into eight and the core removed. Chop a handful of freshly shelled walnuts roughly, and sprinkle them over the pears. Season with a few crushed black peppercorns and a few drops of cider vinegar.

Mascarpone with Fruit

Scoop a large dollop of sweet creamy Mascarpone on to a plate. Surround it with sliced pears, russet apples and a small bunch of muscat grapes. Dip the fruit into the cheese.

Ricotta with Apricots and *Amaretti*

Go for the freshest Ricotta in the deli; it should be soft, crumbly and white. Put a slice in the centre of a plate and eat it with stoned fresh apricots and little Italian almond biscuits, *amaretti*.

Slices of melting baked aubergine with a somewhat Italian bent.
At their most basic, with olive oil and thyme, they make a tender
accompaniment to grilled fish or poultry. A little more imagination
can turn them quite effortlessly into a main dish.

FOR 2

2 medium aubergines
125 g/4 fl oz olive oil
thyme

Set the oven to 200°C/400°F (gas mark 6). Slice the aubergines
about 1 cm/½ inch thick. It does not matter whether you slice
them into rounds or from stem lengthways. Brush a baking sheet
with a little olive oil and arrange the slices on it in one layer. Brush
the slices generously with olive oil. Sprinkle with a little thyme,
though it should be fresh rather than dried, and then with some
salt and coarsely ground pepper.

Bake till tender, about 15–20 minutes.

Three ways with Aubergine Slices

With Tomato Sauce and Parmesan

Spread lavishly with thick tomato sauce and a good sprinkling of
Parmesan cheese, and return to the oven till bubbling.

With Pesto and Mozzarella

Slather ready-made pesto sauce over the baked aubergines, with or without the thyme, and cover with thin slices of Mozzarella cheese. Season the cheese with pepper and a trickle of olive oil, and then grill till the cheese just melts. But no longer lest it toughens.

With Red Peppers and Pine Nuts

Quarter, core and seed 2 red peppers and bake them with the aubergines as above. Dot over a few pine nuts and raisins, grill for a minute to colour the nuts and then scatter with torn mint leaves and coarsely ground black pepper. Serve with thick, cold yoghurt into which you have stirred some more chopped mint.

GRILLED HERBED FIELD MUSHROOMS

FOR 2, AS A STARTER OR LIGHT SUPPER WITH
SALAD, BREAD AND WINE

6 large field mushrooms
a small fistful of parsley and mint, chopped
salt
freshly ground black pepper
4 cloves of garlic, finely sliced
1 wineglass of olive oil

Twist out the stalks from the mushrooms and chop them finely. Wipe the mushrooms and lay them, gill side up, in a baking dish. Mix together the herbs and seasonings and stir in the chopped stalks.

Press the thin slices of garlic here and there into the mushroom caps. Scatter over the herb mixture and then pour the olive oil over the lot. Leave for 10 minutes while you heat the grill.

Grill the mushrooms, spooning over the cooking juices, until they are cooked right through, about 5–7 minutes.

WARM NEW POTATO SALAD WITH MELTED TALEGGIO AND ROCKET

Taleggio is just one of the mild-mannered cheeses that could work well with the pungent flavour of the rocket. Brie or a mildly flavoured Cantal are possibilities.

FOR 2, AS A SUBSTANTIAL SNACK OR LIGHT SUPPER

450 g / 1 lb new potatoes, wiped clean
2 handfuls of rocket, washed and shaken dry
15 ml / 1 tablespoon extra virgin olive oil
200 g / 7 oz mild, semi-soft cheese

Cook the potatoes in boiling salted water until tender to the point of a knife, about 12 minutes.

Toss the leaves in the olive oil and dump on two ovenproof plates. Drain the potatoes and slice each one in half. Scatter them over the salad leaves. Slice the cheese thinly over the potatoes. Set the plate under a preheated grill and cook till the cheese starts to ooze, about 1 minute. Eat immediately.

• *No rocket? Try radicchio and Roquefort, or watercress and Gruyère.*

A plump baked potato with a crisp skin must be on everyone's list of comfort food. On a cold, rainy night the smell of a potato baking must be one of the most appetizing of all. Baked potatoes fit into this collection of 30-minute suppers because of the absurdly small amount of work you need to do to them to make a meal. They take a good hour to cook, but it is an unattended hour, leaving you free to do other things. There is hardly a meal on earth that is less hassle than a baked potato and salad.

The best potatoes for baking are the big floury ones. I have had some success with smaller ones but they lack the majesty of a real whopper. King Edward are very fine; if there are none around, try the common Maris Piper. I am not convinced that the red-skinned Desirée crisp up well, though some people swear by them.

I have exploded many baked potatoes in my time. Sometimes I have opened the oven door to find that just the skins remain, while the flesh has pebble-dashed the inside of my oven. The best way to avoid such potato bombs is to push a metal skewer straight through the middle. This will also cut down the cooking time as the heat travels along the skewer. Failing that, you can prick them all over with a fork to let out the steam.

The potato is done when the skewer pulls out easily and the skin is crisp. The best way to achieve perfection is by ensuring the potatoes are dry and the oven is set to at least 200°C/400°F (gas mark 6). A large potato will take about an hour. When it is cooked cut a cross in the centre and push hard with the fingertips of both hands. The quicker the steam leaves the potato the better the chance of the flesh turning to a lovely fluffy pile.

- *Some of the potatoes sold in plastic bags or clingfilm are very dull. Take a look at the organic offerings. Although they take longer to scrub, as they are usually caked in soil, your hard work may be rewarded by a better flavour.*

I have a notion that cold, sweet, unsalted butter hard from the fridge is nicer than soft room-temperature stuff on a baked potato, but it may, of course, just be my imagination.

A delicious result can be obtained by slicing the potatoes through the horizon, scoring the flesh in lattice fashion, then baking as normal. This method also cuts the cooking time by a third.

When the potato is cooked, try slicing off a 'lid' and scooping out the flesh. Mash it with butter or natural plain yoghurt and anything else you fancy, then stuff it all back into the potato shell. Sit the lid on top if you must.

Sweet potatoes are good too. Bake them in the usual way, putting them on a tray to catch the drips of caramelizing sugar that leak from the sweet orange flesh. They need little in the way of adornment; butter and freshly ground black pepper are the most flattering, I think.

Good things to top a Baked Potato

- Cold butter straight from the fridge
- *Fromage frais*
- Garlic cream cheese, such as Boursin
- Grated Cheddar or Gruyère cheese with chopped fresh flat-leaf parsley and walnuts
- A spoonful of tapenade

- Garlic mayonnaise
- Crushed goat's cheese and shredded baby spinach leaves
- Chicken or duck livers, sautéed in butter and sprinkled with balsamic vinegar
- Thinly sliced Mozzarella and chopped fresh oregano
- Bottled roast peppers, grilled till sweet and slightly charred, then chopped and drizzled with warm extra virgin olive oil and black pepper
- Eat the flesh from the potato then pile a leafy, garlicky salad into the hollow skins
- Mash the flesh with pesto sauce from a bottle and scatter over a little grated Parmesan cheese; toast under the grill till hot
- Sliced avocado and toasted flaked almonds
- Sliced onions, sautéed in butter till sweet and golden
- Streaky bacon cooked till crisp then crumbled with toasted pumpkin seeds and melted butter

TOMATOES WITH MOZZARELLA AND BREADCRUMBS

Plum tomatoes often have more to offer in terms of flavour than other varieties. They also tend to hold their shape better than most, as anyone who has made a sauce with tinned tomatoes will testify. This recipe pushes the 30-minute cook to the limit. It takes about 40.

FOR 4, AS A MAIN DISH

12 plum tomatoes
175 g/6 oz fresh breadcrumbs
8 anchovy fillets, rinsed, dried and chopped

2 plump cloves of garlic, crushed
a handful of parsley, chopped
1 ball of Mozzarella cheese, finely diced
90 ml/6 tablespoons olive oil

Preheat the oven to 220°C/425°F (gas mark 7). Slice the tomatoes in half lengthways and scoop the seeds into a bowl. Place the tomatoes skin side down in a roasting tin so that they nudge up to each other. Mix the tomato scoopings with the breadcrumbs, anchovy fillets, garlic, parsley, Mozzarella and 2 tablespoons of the olive oil.

Season with black pepper and salt, and then pile the filling into the tomato halves. Pour over the remaining olive oil. Bake in the preheated oven for 25 minutes, until the filling is golden.

THAI CHICKEN SALAD

Refreshing, hot, spicy and crisp; and versatile. Swap the sliced, crisp, skinned chicken for duck, pork belly, squid or prawns if you wish.

A SUBSTANTIAL SUPPER FOR 2

1 large (or 2 smaller) boned chicken or duck breast
olive oil
60 ml/4 tablespoons lime juice
30 ml/2 tablespoons fish sauce (nam pla)
15 ml/1 tablespoon light soy sauce
60 ml/4 tablespoons groundnut oil
a little sesame oil
5 ml/1 teaspoon sugar

1 garlic clove, finely sliced
15 ml/1 tablespoon chopped mint
½ cucumber, peeled
1 large carrot, scrubbed
small handful coriander leaves
1 hot red chilli pepper, seeded and cut into fine shreds
1 red onion, finely chopped
2 handfuls of bean sprouts, washed

Grill the chicken or duck breast, brushed with a little oil and seasoned with salt and pepper, till tender. The skin should be crisp. You can sauté it if you prefer. Slice into 1 cm/½ inch strips.

While the chicken is grilling, mix the lime juice, *nam pla*, soy and groundnut oil. Stir in a shake or two of sesame oil. Go easy as it is inclined to overpower everything else. Stir in the sugar, garlic and the chopped mint. Season with freshly ground black pepper. No salt.

Slice the cucumber and carrot finely. A vegetable peeler will be ten times quicker than a knife. Just run the peeler up or down the vegetables, shaving off long thin slices. It's quite fun actually. In a large bowl, toss the dressing with the cucumber and carrot shavings, the coriander and chilli, the onion and the bean sprouts. Toss in the chicken or duck. Serve immediately.

COUSCOUS NIÇOISE

FOR 2

125 g/4 oz French beans, cut in half lengthways
225 g/8 oz couscous

4 tomatoes, ripe but firm
10 black olives, stoned and halved
4 anchovy fillets, rinsed
a large handful of flat-leaf parsley, chopped
30 ml/2 tablespoons chopped coriander leaves
lemon wedges, to serve

For the dressing:

1 plump young clove of garlic, crushed to a paste
45 ml/3 tablespoons extra virgin olive oil
5 ml/1 teaspoon lemon juice

Cook the beans in boiling salted water till they are bright green and tender, about 6 minutes. They are there to add crunch to the soft grain, so cook them slightly less than you would for a vegetable accompaniment. Drain and run cold water through them to stop them cooking.

Meanwhile, soak the couscous with a little water, about 150 ml/ ¼ pint will be enough although it will not appear so at first. Leave for about 10 minutes and then crumble the lumps that form between your fingers. When the grain has swelled a little, stir in the cooked beans, the tomatoes cut into small dice, and the olives, anchovies and herbs.

Make the dressing by whisking together the ingredients and seasoning generously with salt and freshly ground black pepper. Toss the salad with the dressing, set aside for 10 minutes, or longer if you have it, and then serve with lemon wedges.

GRILLED PEPPERS WITH BALSAMIC
VINEGAR AND BASIL

There is an exciting mixture of flavours here. The whole point of grilling the peppers is to release their sweet, smoky juices and exploit them in the warm dressing with the deep sweet-sour richness of balsamic vinegar. The resulting sweetness is then balanced by the basil and lemon.

FOR 2

> *2 medium red peppers*
> *1 aubergine, weighing about 225 g/8 oz*
> *1 medium onion, peeled*
> *4 bushy sprigs of thyme*
> *2 plump cloves of garlic, crushed*
> *175 ml/6 fl oz extra virgin olive oil*
> *salt*
> *freshly ground black pepper*
> *2 large plum tomatoes, halved and cut into thick slices*
> *1 tablespoon balsamic vinegar*
> *juice of ½ lemon*
> *a small handful of basil leaves, shredded*

Cut the peppers in half through the stalk, then pull out and discard anything that isn't red. Put the halves in a grill pan, on the base rather than the wire mesh, with their cut sides down. Halve the aubergine lengthways, cut each half into 5 mm/¼ inch thick slices and put in a bowl.

Cut the onion horizontally in slices no thicker than pound coins. Separate the rings and add them to the aubergine. Strip

the leaves from the thyme branches, add to the onion and aubergine with the garlic and pour over the olive oil. Grind over
a little black pepper and salt, then toss together the vegetables
and thyme with a spoon making sure they are all covered with
oil.

Scatter them over the rest of the grill pan and cook under a
preheated grill, about 7.5 – 10 cm/3 – 4 inches from the heat. When
the pepper skins start to blacken, turn them over. Stir the aubergine
mixture around as it starts to brown. After 15 minutes' cooking,
add the tomatoes. Continue grilling until the aubergines and onion
are tender, and the peppers have lightly charred skins and soft,
but far from collapsing, flesh – about a further 10 – 12 minutes.

Remove the pan from the grill and carefully spoon out the pan
juices into the bowl in which you mixed the vegetables. Whisk in
the balsamic vinegar, lemon juice and shredded basil with a fork.
Taste for seasoning; you may need a bit more salt and pepper.
Place the peppers on warm plates and stuff with the grilled
vegetables. Spoon over the warm dressing and eat straight away.
Eat with crusty bread to mop up the juices.

BROCCOLI AND MUSHROOM STIR-FRY

A classic Chinese stir-fry. Nothing fancy. Unless you want to
throw in some smarter mushrooms such as shiitake or oyster. The
best version of this I have yet made used big black mushrooms
(they had been around a day or two) and a slice of lamb's liver,
added with the mushrooms.

225 g/8 oz chestnut or large flat mushrooms, wiped
45 ml/3 tablespoons groundnut oil
4 spring onions, chopped
2 large cloves of garlic, sliced
225 g/8 oz broccoli stems and florets, cut into bite-sized
 pieces
30 ml/2 tablespoons light soy sauce
30 ml/2 tablespoons rice wine or dry sherry

If you are using brown cup mushrooms, cut them into quarters; if you have large flat ones, slice them about as thick as pound coins. Heat a wok. Get it really quite hot and then pour in the oil. Straight away add the spring onions and cook till they wilt and turn dark green, a minute or so; then add the garlic and cook for a minute till dark golden brown.

Stir in the broccoli and fry for 2 minutes, stirring almost continuously, till it turns vivid green. Add the mushrooms with a little more oil if the broccoli has drunk it all. Fry for 2 minutes then add the soy sauce and rice wine or sherry. Fry and stir the whole lot for a minute or two till the broccoli is tender and the mushrooms brown. Season with freshly ground pepper. You won't need salt with all that soy. Serve hot and sizzling from the pan.

SPINACH WITH BLUE CHEESE AND PASTA

Any soft blue-veined cheese will be right for this. There is little point in using a great cheese, such as Gorgonzola or Irish Cashel Blue, unless you have some to use up. A Dolcelatte or blue Brie is quite adequate. I like to follow this rich and almost instant dish with a plate of salad leaves to mop up the cheesy sauce, lamb's lettuce if I happen to have some, or just some floppy-leaved lettuce.

ENOUGH FOR 2, AS A MAIN DISH WITH A SALAD
   TO FOLLOW

280 g/10 oz fresh pasta, any curled or ribbon shape
2 double handfuls of spinach leaves, washed and
   torn up
175 g/6 oz soft, blue cheese, cut into cubes
300 ml/½ pint single cream
salt
freshly ground black pepper

Cook the pasta, uncovered, in salted, boiling water till *al dente*. Put the spinach, still wet from washing, in a pan over a medium heat. Cover with a lid, and cook till it starts to wilt, a matter of 2 minutes or so. Add the blue cheese and the cream. Cook over a gentle heat until the cheese melts into the cream. Taste it and then season accordingly, remembering that some blue cheeses are a little salty.

When the cheese has melted and the spinach is still bright green, drain the pasta and fold it into the sauce. Eat hot.

BAKED BANANAS WITH PASSION FRUIT

Hot bananas have a seductive richness about them – some might say too rich. The tart passion fruit serves the purpose of contrasting that richness and offering one of the most fragrant fast puddings imaginable.

FOR 4

4 ripe bananas, peeled
30 ml / 2 tablespoons runny honey
a little lemon juice
juice of ½ orange
6 passion fruits

Wrap up each banana in kitchen foil leaving the top open. The easy way to do this is to place the foil flat on a work surface. Place a banana on each one, then bring up the sides of the foil to make little packets for the fruit. Drizzle the honey over the bananas. Squeeze a little lemon juice in each packet and then drizzle over the orange juice. Cut the passion fruit in half and squeeze four of the halves over the banana parcels.

Scrunch together the foil at the top to seal. Bake in a preheated oven at 200°C/400°F (gas mark 6) for about 20 minutes. Test for doneness with a skewer. Put the parcels on to plates and hand round. Give everyone two halves of a passion fruit. Each diner should squeeze their passion fruit on to their bananas as they open the packet. The scent will be exquisite.

• *A passion fruit is ripe when it is severely wrinkled. But it should still weigh heavy in the hand. That is a sign that it is full of juice.*

THE TWENTY-MINUTE RICE PUDDING

A creamy rice pudding in less time than it takes to heat up a ready-made one. There are tinned ones, of course, but the rice is too soft and pappy. Pudding or *arborio* (risotto) rice is essential if the grains are to swell up in juicy fashion.

FOR 4

8 heaped tablespoons arborio *or pudding rice*
300 ml / ½ pint milk
300 ml / ½ pint double cream
a vanilla pod, split in half lengthways or 1 teaspoon
    vanilla extract
90 ml / 6 tablespoons water
large knob of butter
4 tablespoons caster sugar

Put the rice in a medium-sized, heavy-based pan, then pour in the milk, cream, vanilla pod or extract and water. Bring to the boil over a medium heat, then turn down the flame until the milk is bubbling gently, just as you would have it for a risotto.

Let it cook for 15–20 minutes until the rice has swelled with the milk. It should be soft when done, but not without a little bite. Add the butter, no more than an ounce, whip out the vanilla pod, and stir in the sugar. As soon as the sugar has dissolved, the pudding is ready.

HOT PEACHES WITH MASCARPONE AND PINE NUTS

FOR 2

4 ripe peaches
60 ml / 4 tablespoons Mascarpone cheese
30 ml / 2 tablespoons pine nuts

Cut the peaches in half and remove the stones. Put the peaches in a shallow ovenproof dish, flat side up. Dot half a tablespoon of 51

Mascarpone in the hollow of each peach. Scatter pine nuts over the cheese and place under a preheated hot grill till the cheese has melted and the pine nuts are golden.

TEN-MINUTE TRIFLE

Real trifle, made with home-made sponge cake, syllabub and a gallon of sherry must be one of the most delicious puddings known to man, but it takes an age to make from scratch. The commercial alternative contains lurid orange jelly topped with a substance akin to shaving foam, only sweeter. It is topped with rainbow-coloured sugar-strands, or if you are really unlucky, those teeth-breaking silver balls.

The following recipe is almost as quick as its name and has some of the alcoholic creaminess of the former without any of the horrors, not to mention the E numbers, of the latter. I serve it unadorned, just a soft creamy mass in a plain bowl, scattering crystallized violets or rose petals over the surface only if I am feeling tacky.

FOR 4, AND IT IS EVEN BETTER THE NEXT DAY

10 sponge fingers, broken into 2.5-cm/1-inch pieces
255 ml/8 fl oz chilled sweet white wine, such as Moscato
  or half sherry
125 g/4 oz raspberries, loganberries or juicy blackberries
2 ripe bananas, peeled and sliced
2 eggs, separated
50 g/2 oz caster sugar
225 g/8 oz Mascarpone cheese
a little vanilla extract or brandy

Put the sponge fingers in a 1.1-litre/2-pint dish. You can use that cut-glass thing Auntie Connie gave you if you must, but the trifle looks far more elegant in a plain white china bowl. Pour over the wine, gently pressing the fingers down into the liquid, then throw in the raspberries or other berries and the bananas.

Cream the egg yolks with the sugar, add the Mascarpone and beat with an electric whisk till light and creamy. Tip in the vanilla or brandy. Whisk the egg whites till they form stiff peaks and fold gently but thoroughly into the cream. Tip the Mascarpone cream over the fruit and sponge. Shake the bowl gently for a few seconds. Set aside for as long as you can. A minute should suffice.

PENGUIN 60s

ISABEL ALLENDE · *Voices in My Ear*
NICHOLSON BAKER · *Playing Trombone*
LINDSEY BAREHAM · *The Little Book of Big Soups*
KAREN BLIXEN · *From the Ngong Hills*
DIRK BOGARDE · *Coming of Age*
ANTHONY BURGESS · *Childhood*
ANGELA CARTER · *Lizzie Borden*
CARLOS CASTANEDA · *The Sorcerer's Ring of Power*
ELIZABETH DAVID · *Peperonata and Other Italian Dishes*
RICHARD DAWKINS · *The Pocket Watchmaker*
GERALD DURRELL · *The Pageant of Fireflies*
RICHARD ELLMANN · *The Trial of Oscar Wilde*
EPICURUS · *Letter on Happiness*
MARIANNE FAITHFULL · *Year One*
KEITH FLOYD · *Hot and Spicy Floyd*
ALEXANDER FRATER · *Where the Dawn Comes Up Like Thunder*
ESTHER FREUD · *Meeting Bilal*
JOHN KENNETH GALBRAITH · *The Culture of Contentment*
ROB GRANT AND DOUG NAYLOR · *Scenes from the Dwarf*
ROBERT GRAVES · *The Gods of Olympus*
JANE GRIGSON · *Puddings*
SOPHIE GRIGSON · *From Sophie's Table*
KATHARINE HEPBURN · *Little Me*
SUSAN HILL · *The Badness Within Him*
ALAN HOLLINGHURST · *Adventures Underground*
BARRY HUMPHRIES · *Less is More.Please*
HOWARD JACOBSON · *Expulsion from Paradise*
P. D. JAMES · *The Girl Who Loved Graveyards*
STEPHEN KING · *Umney's Last Case*
LAO TZU · *Tao Te Ching*
DAVID LEAVITT · *Chips Is Here*

PENGUIN 60s

LAURIE LEE · *To War in Spain*

PATRICK LEIGH FERMOR · *Loose as the Wind*

ELMORE LEONARD · *Trouble at Rindo's Station*

DAVID LODGE · *Surprised by Summer*

BERNARD MAC LAVERTY · *The Miraculous Candidate*

SHENA MACKAY · *Cloud-Cuckoo-Land*

NORMAN MAILER · *The Dressing Room*

PETER MAYLE · *Postcards from Summer*

JAN MORRIS · *Scenes from Havian Life*

BLAKE MORRISON · *Camp Cuba*

VLADIMIR NABOKOV · *Now Remember*

REDMOND O'HANLON · *A River in Borneo*

STEVEN PINKER · *Thinking in Tongues*

CRAIG RAINE · *Private View*

CLAUDIA RODEN · *Ful Medames and Other Vegetarian Dishes*

HELGE RUBINSTEIN · *Chocolate Parfait*

SIMON SCHAMA · *The Taking of the Bastille*

WILL SELF · *The Rock of Crack As Big As the Ritz*

MARK SHAND · *Elephant Tales*

NIGEL SLATER · *30-Minute Suppers*

RICK STEIN · *Fresh from the Sea*

LYTTON STRACHEY · *Florence Nightingale*

PAUL THEROUX · *Slow Trains to Simla*

COLIN THUBRON · *Samarkand*

MARK TULLY · *Beyond Purdah*

LAURENS VAN DER POST · *Merry Christmas, Mr Lawrence*

MARGARET VISSER · *More than Meets the Eye*

GAVIN YOUNG · *Something of Samoa*

and

Thirty Obituaries from Wisden · SELECTED BY MATTHEW ENGEL

READ MORE IN PENGUIN

For complete information about books available from Penguin and how to order them, please write to us at the appropriate address below. Please note that for copyright reasons the selection of books varies from country to country.

IN THE UNITED KINGDOM: Please write to *Dept. EP, Penguin Books Ltd, Bath Road, Harmondsworth, Middlesex UB7 0DA.*

IN THE UNITED STATES: Please write to *Consumer Sales, Penguin USA, P.O. Box 999, Dept. 17109, Bergenfield, New Jersey 07621-0120.* VISA and MasterCard holders call 1-800-253-6476 to order Penguin titles.

IN CANADA: Please write to *Penguin Books Canada Ltd, 10 Alcorn Avenue, Suite 300, Toronto, Ontario M4V 3B2.*

IN AUSTRALIA: Please write to *Penguin Books Australia Ltd, P.O. Box 257, Ringwood, Victoria 3134.*

IN NEW ZEALAND: Please write to *Penguin Books (NZ) Ltd, Private Bag 102902, North Shore Mail Centre, Auckland 10.*

IN INDIA: Please write to *Penguin Books India Pvt Ltd, 706 Eros Apartments, 56 Nehru Place, New Delhi 110 019.*

IN THE NETHERLANDS: Please write to *Penguin Books Netherlands bv, Postbus 3507, NL-1001 AH Amsterdam.*

IN GERMANY: Please write to *Penguin Books Deutschland GmbH, Metzlerstrasse 26, 60594 Frankfurt am Main.*

IN SPAIN: Please write to *Penguin Books S. A., Bravo Murillo 19, 1° B, 28015 Madrid.*

IN ITALY: Please write to *Penguin Italia s.r.l., Via Felice Casati 20, I-20124 Milano.*

IN FRANCE: Please write to *Penguin France S. A., 17 rue Lejeune, F-31000 Toulouse.*

IN JAPAN: Please write to *Penguin Books Japan, Ishikiribashi Building, 2-5-4, Suido, Bunkyo-ku, Tokyo 112.*

IN GREECE: Please write to *Penguin Hellas Ltd, Dimocritou 3, GR-106 71 Athens.*

IN SOUTH AFRICA: Please write to *Longman Penguin Southern Africa (Pty) Ltd, Private Bag X08, Bertsham 2013.*